Writing Addition Problems

This is an addition **equation** (problem).
The answer is called the **sum**.

 $\underline{}3\underline{} + \underline{}4\underline{} = \underline{}7\underline{}$

Use the pictures below to help you write an **equation** and its **sum**.

1.   _____ + _____ = _____

2.   _____ + _____ = _____

3.   _____ + _____ = _____

4.   _____ + _____ = _____

5.   _____ + _____ = _____

6.   _____ + _____ = _____

7.   _____ + _____ = _____

Addition Using Fast Doubles

Fast Doubles make adding easier.

Learn these **fast doubles** so you can say them as *fast* as you can!

1 + 1 = 2	4 + 4 = 8	7 + 7 = 14
2 + 2 = 4	5 + 5 = 10	8 + 8 = 16
3 + 3 = 6	6 + 6 = 12	9 + 9 = 18

Octopus

Now try these **fast double** equations. Write the sums as *fast* as you can!

1. 3 + 3 = _____   2 + 2 = _____   5 + 5 = _____

2. 1 + 1 = _____   6 + 6 = _____   8 + 8 = _____

3. 4 + 4 = _____   7 + 7 = _____   9 + 9 = _____

4. 6 + 6 = _____   3 + 3 = _____   1 + 1 = _____

5. 2 + 2 = _____   4 + 4 = _____   7 + 7 = _____

Fast Doubles Plus One

Fast Doubles Plus One are just
Fast Doubles with *one* more.

$2 + 2 + 1 = \mathbf{5}$ $2 + 3 = \mathbf{5}$

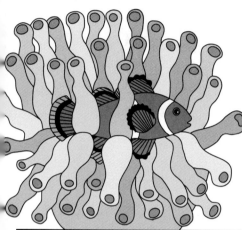

Learn these fast **doubles plus one**.
They're easy if you know your **fast doubles**.

$1 + 2 = 3$	$4 + 5 = 9$	$7 + 8 = 15$
$2 + 3 = 5$	$5 + 6 = 11$	$8 + 9 = 17$
$3 + 4 = 7$	$6 + 7 = 13$	

Clown Anemonefish

Practice the **fast doubles plus one**.

1. $4 + 5 = $ _____ $1 + 2 = $ _____ $3 + 4 = $ _____

2. $6 + 7 = $ _____ $2 + 3 = $ _____ $8 + 9 = $ _____

3. $7 + 8 = $ _____ $3 + 4 = $ _____ $6 + 7 = $ _____

4. $8 + 9 = $ _____ $4 + 5 = $ _____ $2 + 3 = $ _____

Good Job!

5. $1 + 2 = $ _____ $6 + 7 = $ _____ $8 + 9 = $ _____

Addition Equation Practice

Find the **sums** of the addition equations below.
Look for **fast doubles** and **fast doubles plus one**.

Sperm Whale

1. **3 + 3 =** _____   **3 + 4 =** _____   **5 + 5 =** _____

2. **5 + 6 =** _____   **7 + 7 =** _____   **7 + 8 =** _____

3. **4 + 4 =** _____   **4 + 5 =** _____   **8 + 8 =** _____

4. **8 + 9 =** _____   **2 + 3 =** _____   **6 + 6 =** _____

5. **6 + 7 =** _____   **9 + 9 =** _____   **7 + 8 =** _____

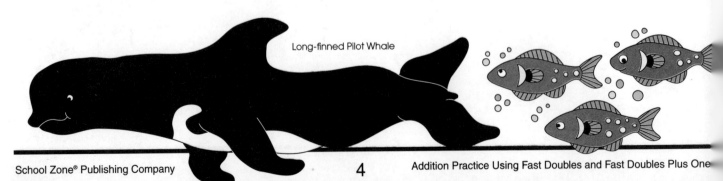

Long-finned Pilot Whale

More Addition Facts to Practice

Circle each equation that gives the correct answer.

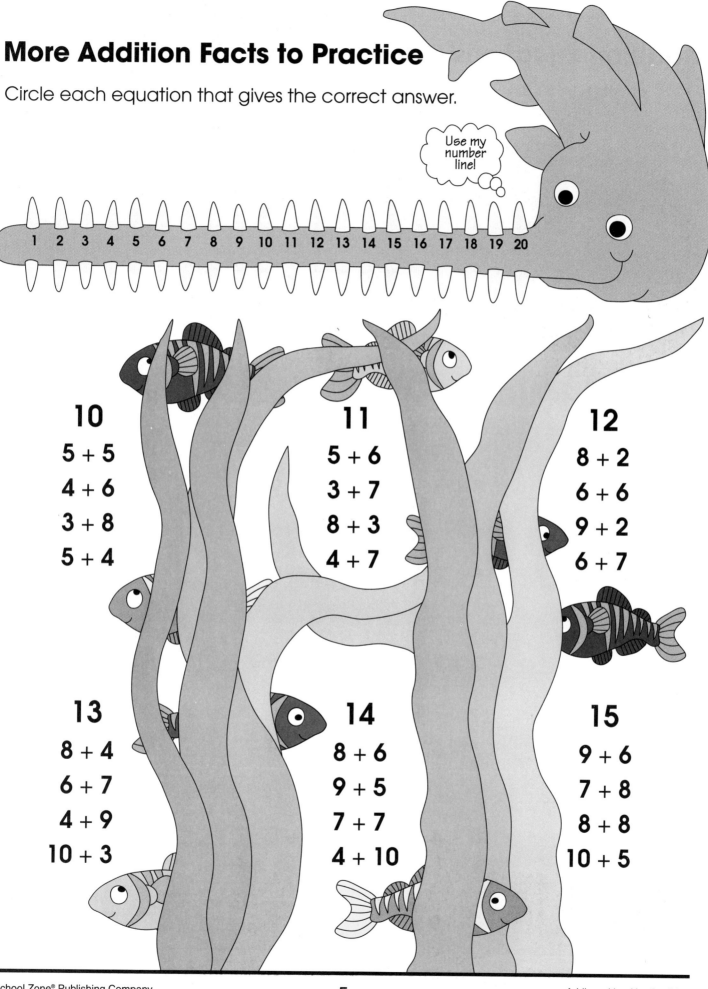

Use my number line!

1 2 3 4 5 6 7 8 9 10 11 12 13 14 15 16 17 18 19 20

10
5 + 5
4 + 6
3 + 8
5 + 4

11
5 + 6
3 + 7
8 + 3
4 + 7

12
8 + 2
6 + 6
9 + 2
6 + 7

13
8 + 4
6 + 7
4 + 9
10 + 3

14
8 + 6
9 + 5
7 + 7
4 + 10

15
9 + 6
7 + 8
8 + 8
10 + 5

Addition Equations Can Be Turned Around!

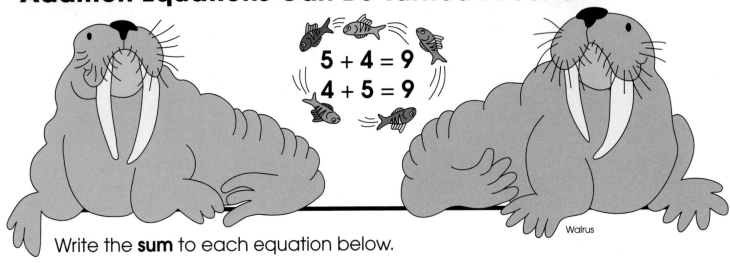

$5 + 4 = 9$
$4 + 5 = 9$

Walrus

Write the **sum** to each equation below.

1. $5 + 6 =$ _____ $6 + 5 =$ _____ $6 + 8 =$ _____ $8 + 6 =$ _____

2. $4 + 7 =$ _____ $7 + 4 =$ _____ $8 + 9 =$ _____ $9 + 8 =$ _____

3. $8 + 5 =$ _____ $5 + 8 =$ _____ $4 + 9 =$ _____ $9 + 4 =$ _____

4. $7 + 3 =$ _____ $3 + 7 =$ _____ $7 + 5 =$ _____ $5 + 7 =$ _____

5. $6 + 7 =$ _____ $7 + 6 =$ _____ $6 + 9 =$ _____ $9 + 6 =$ _____

6. $4 + 8 =$ _____ $8 + 4 =$ _____ $3 + 8 =$ _____ $8 + 3 =$ _____

7. $9 + 7 =$ _____ $7 + 9 =$ _____ $7 + 2 =$ _____ $2 + 7 =$ _____

More Practice on Addition Equations

Add to finish the problems.

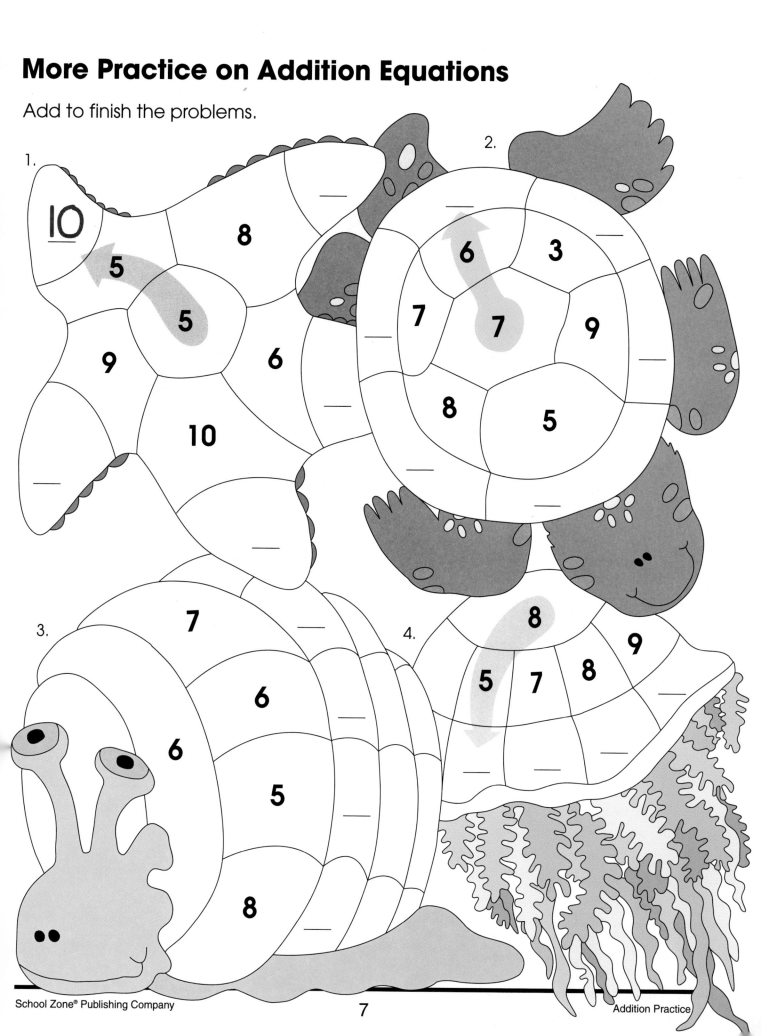

1.

2.

3.

4.

Adding Three Addends

To add three numerals (**addends**) together you:

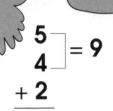

1. Add the **5 + 4** and the sum is **9**.

2. Then add the sum of **9** to the **2**

   and the sum is **11**.

$$\left.\begin{array}{r} 5 \\ 4 \end{array}\right] = 9$$
$$\begin{array}{r} +\ 2 \\ \hline 11 \end{array}$$

Find the **sum**.

1.
$$\begin{array}{r} 2 \\ 6 \\ +\ 7 \\ \hline \end{array} \qquad \begin{array}{r} 5 \\ 8 \\ +\ 3 \\ \hline \end{array} \qquad \begin{array}{r} 9 \\ 4 \\ +\ 4 \\ \hline \end{array} \qquad \begin{array}{r} 3 \\ 4 \\ +\ 8 \\ \hline \end{array}$$

2.
$$\begin{array}{r} 4 \\ 7 \\ +\ 6 \\ \hline \end{array} \qquad \begin{array}{r} 6 \\ 6 \\ +\ 2 \\ \hline \end{array} \qquad \begin{array}{r} 3 \\ 1 \\ +\ 7 \\ \hline \end{array} \qquad \begin{array}{r} 5 \\ 5 \\ +\ 8 \\ \hline \end{array}$$

3.
$$\begin{array}{r} 2 \\ 3 \\ +\ 6 \\ \hline \end{array} \qquad \begin{array}{r} 7 \\ 4 \\ +\ 4 \\ \hline \end{array} \qquad \begin{array}{r} 8 \\ 2 \\ +\ 5 \\ \hline \end{array} \qquad \begin{array}{r} 1 \\ 8 \\ +\ 8 \\ \hline \end{array}$$

Subtraction Equations

The answer to a subtraction equation is called the **difference**.

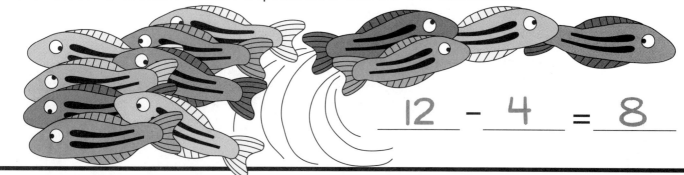

12 – 4 = 8

Write your own subtraction equations and their **differences**.

1.  _____ – _____ = _____

2.  _____ – _____ = _____

3.  _____ – _____ = _____

4. _____ – _____ = _____

5.  _____ – _____ = _____

6.  _____ – _____ = _____

7. _____ – _____ = _____

Subtraction and Addition Are Part of a Family

Subtraction is the **opposite** of **addition**. If you know addition facts, you can figure out the answer to a subtraction equation.

Fill in the blanks to make the family correct.

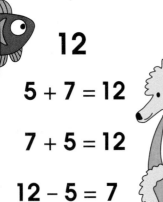

12

$5 + 7 = 12$

$7 + 5 = 12$

$12 - 5 = 7$

$12 - 7 = 5$

13

$\underline{} + 9 = 13$

$9 + 4 = \underline{}$

$13 - \underline{} = 9$

$13 - \underline{} = 4$

14

$8 + 6 = \underline{}$

$6 + \underline{} = 14$

$14 - 8 = \underline{}$

$14 - 6 = \underline{}$

15

$8 + \underline{} = 15$

$7 + 8 = \underline{}$

$15 - \underline{} = 7$

$15 - \underline{} = 8$

16

$\underline{} + 7 = 16$

$7 + 9 = \underline{}$

$16 - 9 = \underline{}$

$16 - 7 = \underline{}$

17

$8 + \underline{} = 17$

$9 + 8 = \underline{}$

$17 - \underline{} = 9$

$17 - \underline{} = 8$

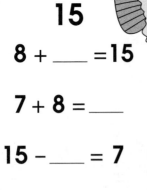

Subtraction: Fast Doubles and Fast Doubles Plus One

Subtraction fast doubles are the opposite of addition fast doubles.

$$10 - 5 = \underline{5}$$

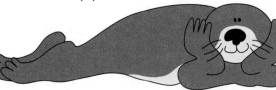

5 + 5 = 10
10 − 5 = 5

Fast doubles plus one in subtraction are the opposite, too.

$$13 - 6 = \underline{7}$$

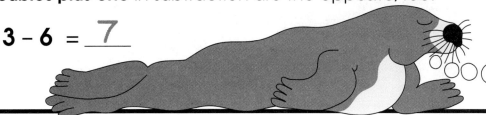

6 + 6 + 1 = 13
13 − 6 = 6 + 1

If you get stuck on the answer to the subtraction problems below, think about fast doubles and fast doubles **plus one**.

1.
$$\begin{array}{r} 14 \\ -\ 7 \\ \hline \end{array}$$
$$\begin{array}{r} 18 \\ -\ 9 \\ \hline \end{array}$$
$$\begin{array}{r} 12 \\ -\ 6 \\ \hline \end{array}$$
$$\begin{array}{r} 13 \\ -\ 6 \\ \hline \end{array}$$
$$\begin{array}{r} 17 \\ -\ 8 \\ \hline \end{array}$$

2.
$$\begin{array}{r} 10 \\ -\ 5 \\ \hline \end{array}$$
$$\begin{array}{r} 15 \\ -\ 7 \\ \hline \end{array}$$
$$\begin{array}{r} 9 \\ -\ 4 \\ \hline \end{array}$$
$$\begin{array}{r} 16 \\ -\ 8 \\ \hline \end{array}$$
$$\begin{array}{r} 13 \\ -\ 6 \\ \hline \end{array}$$

Watch out for these!
They are **opposites** of fast doubles and fast doubles **plus one**.

3.
$$\begin{array}{r} 13 \\ -\ 7 \\ \hline \end{array}$$
$$\begin{array}{r} 15 \\ -\ 8 \\ \hline \end{array}$$
$$\begin{array}{r} 17 \\ -\ 9 \\ \hline \end{array}$$
$$\begin{array}{r} 11 \\ -\ 6 \\ \hline \end{array}$$
$$\begin{array}{r} 14 \\ -\ 7 \\ \hline \end{array}$$

More Practice

Find the missing number to each equation below.
Remember fast doubles, fast doubles plus one, opposites and families.

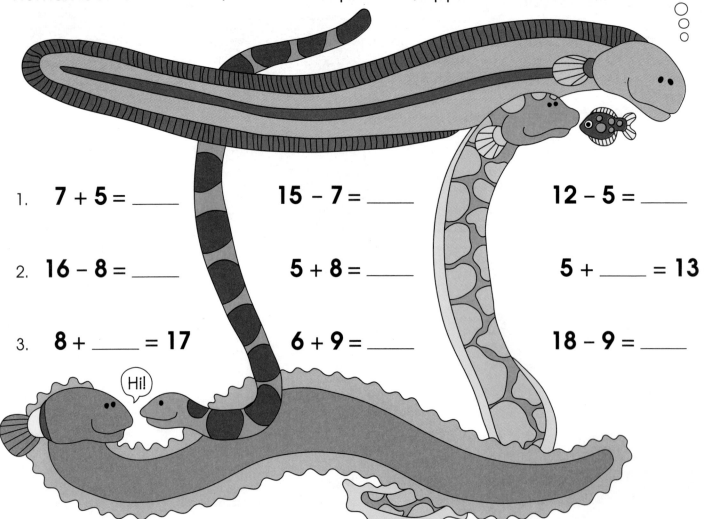

1. $7 + 5 = \underline{\hspace{1cm}}$

$15 - 7 = \underline{\hspace{1cm}}$

$12 - 5 = \underline{\hspace{1cm}}$

2. $16 - 8 = \underline{\hspace{1cm}}$

$5 + 8 = \underline{\hspace{1cm}}$

$5 + \underline{\hspace{1cm}} = 13$

3. $8 + \underline{\hspace{1cm}} = 17$

$6 + 9 = \underline{\hspace{1cm}}$

$18 - 9 = \underline{\hspace{1cm}}$

Hi!

4.
$$\begin{array}{r} 7 \\ + 8 \\ \hline \end{array} \qquad \begin{array}{r} 5 \\ + 8 \\ \hline \end{array} \qquad \begin{array}{r} 3 \\ + 9 \\ \hline \end{array} \qquad \begin{array}{r} 12 \\ - 8 \\ \hline \end{array} \qquad \begin{array}{r} 16 \\ - 7 \\ \hline \end{array}$$

5.
$$\begin{array}{r} 13 \\ - 5 \\ \hline \end{array} \qquad \begin{array}{r} 5 \\ + \boxed{} \\ \hline 11 \end{array} \qquad \begin{array}{r} 7 \\ + 5 \\ \hline \end{array} \qquad \begin{array}{r} 4 \\ + \boxed{} \\ \hline 12 \end{array} \qquad \begin{array}{r} 11 \\ - 3 \\ \hline \end{array}$$

Subtraction Using a Number Line

You can use a number line to find the difference.

The difference of **13 – 7 = 6.**

Flying Fish

| 0 | 1 | 2 | 3 | 4 | 5 | 6 | 7 | 8 | 9 | 10 | 11 | 12 | 13 | 14 | 15 | 16 | 17 | 18 | 19 | 20 |

Now it's your turn to try the problems below.

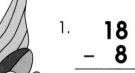

1.
$$\begin{array}{r} 18 \\ -\ 8 \\ \hline \end{array} \qquad \begin{array}{r} 15 \\ -\ 7 \\ \hline \end{array} \qquad \begin{array}{r} 12 \\ -\ 4 \\ \hline \end{array} \qquad \begin{array}{r} 15 \\ -\ 9 \\ \hline \end{array} \qquad \begin{array}{r} 13 \\ -\ 7 \\ \hline \end{array}$$

2.
$$\begin{array}{r} 17 \\ -\ 8 \\ \hline \end{array} \qquad \begin{array}{r} 14 \\ -\ 7 \\ \hline \end{array} \qquad \begin{array}{r} 12 \\ -\ 5 \\ \hline \end{array} \qquad \begin{array}{r} 16 \\ -\ 9 \\ \hline \end{array} \qquad \begin{array}{r} 17 \\ -\ 6 \\ \hline \end{array}$$

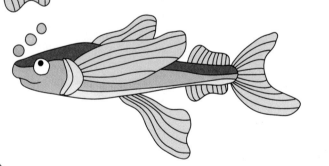

3. **13 – 8 = _____**   **16 – 8 = _____**   **14 – 4 = _____**

4. **10 – 7 = _____**   **11 – 5 = _____**   **18 – 9 = _____**

More Addition and Subtraction Practice

Write the correct missing number for each equation.

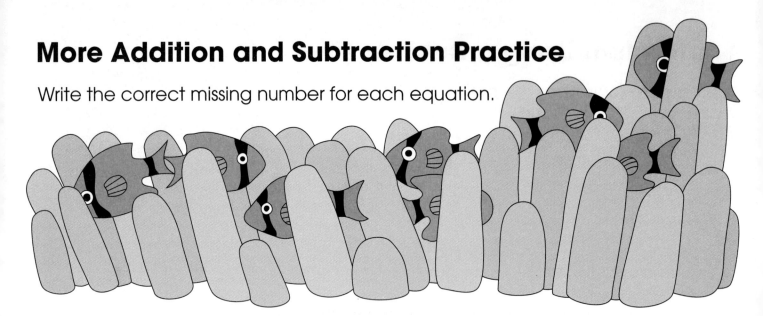

1.   **7 + 3 = _____**   **5 + 6 = _____**   **8 + 9 = _____**

2.   **12 − 8 = _____**   **18 − 9 = _____**   **15 − 8 = _____**

3.   **8 + _____ = 15**   **11 − _____ = 2**   **5 + _____ = 15**

4.   **13 − 8 = _____**   **14 − 8 = _____**   **13 − 7 = _____**

Skate   Atlantic Guitarfish   Atlantic Torpedo

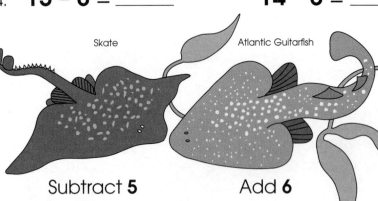

Subtract **5**	Add **6**	Subtract **7**	Add **8**
10 _5_	8 ___	14 ___	6 ___
13 ___	5 ___	15 ___	8 ___
11 ___	9 ___	11 ___	11 ___
14 ___	7 ___	9 ___	9 ___

Adding Tens and Ones

1. Add the **ones**.

Tens	Ones
5	3
+	4
	7

2. Add the **tens**.

Tens	Ones
5	3
+	4
5	7

Add the **ones**.
Then add the **tens**.

1.
Tens	Ones
6	3
+	4

91
+ 8

50
+ 5

2.
78
+ 1

25
+ 3

83
+ 6

3.
45
+ 34

27
+ 70

44
+ 42

4.
32
+ 66

56
+ 53

37
+ 32

Jellyfish

More Tens and Ones to Add

Solve this riddle.

What animal can fit an elephant on its tongue?

REMEMBER: Add the **ones** and then the **tens**!

It's not a goldfish.

G	C	T	W
56	71	43	20
+ 30	+ 25	+ 35	+ 74

A	J	R	G
81	90	85	34
+ 14	+ 7	+ 14	+ 30

U	E	H	L
20	17	55	62
+ 61	+ 42	+ 11	+ 6

W	L	E	B
47	21	40	26
+ 30	+ 4	+ 30	+ 23

49	25	81	70	94	66	95	68	59

Subtracting Tens and Ones

1. Subtract the **ones**.

```
     Tens Ones
       4   9
   -       5
   ─────────
           4
```

2. Subtract the **tens**.

```
     Tens Ones
       4   9
   -       5
   ─────────
       4   4
```

Subtract the **ones**.
Then subtract the **tens**.

```
   Tens Ones
```

1.
```
    57        45        69
  -  2      -  3      -  7
  ─────     ─────     ─────
```

2.
```
    78        24        98
  -  5      -  3      -  6
  ─────     ─────     ─────
```

3.
```
    47        66        89
  - 22      - 43      - 26
  ─────     ─────     ─────
```

4.
```
    59        76        99
  - 23      - 34      - 47
  ─────     ─────     ─────
```

More Tens and Ones to Subtract

REMEMBER: Subtract the **ones** and then the **tens**!

Giant Squid

1.
$$58 - 26$$ $$86 - 2$$ $$99 - 56$$

2.
$$77 - 40$$ $$45 - 14$$ $$26 - 5$$

3.
$$38 - 15$$ $$67 - 36$$ $$53 - 31$$

4.
$$85 - 52$$ $$78 - 6$$ $$37 - 30$$

5.
$$59 - 40$$ $$76 - 34$$ $$87 - 2$$

Adding Tens and Ones and Regrouping

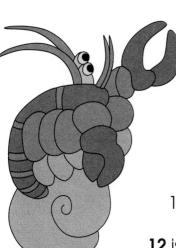

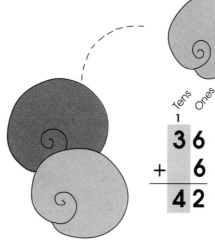

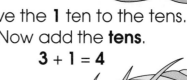

```
     Tens  Ones
       3  6
    +     6
    ─────────
       1  2
```

```
          1
     Tens  Ones
       3  6
    +     6
    ─────────
       4  2
```

1. Add the **ones**.
6 + 6 = 12
12 is **1 ten** and **2 ones**.

2. Give the **1** ten to the tens.
Now add the **tens**.
3 + 1 = 4

Add the equations below.
Be sure to **regroup**.

Hermit Crab

```
     Tens  Ones
```

1.
```
    56          24          89
  +  7        +  9        +  3
  ─────       ─────       ─────
```

2.
```
    28          45          37
  +  4        +  7        +  7
  ─────       ─────       ─────
```

3.
```
    57          48          64
  +  5        +  8        +  6
  ─────       ─────       ─────
```

Practice Adding with Regrouping

Add the equations.

Mako Shark

Hammerhead Shark

1.
$$\begin{array}{r} 58 \\ + 4 \\ \hline \end{array}$$
$$\begin{array}{r} 24 \\ + 7 \\ \hline \end{array}$$
$$\begin{array}{r} 36 \\ + 4 \\ \hline \end{array}$$
$$\begin{array}{r} 75 \\ + 6 \\ \hline \end{array}$$

2.
$$\begin{array}{r} 48 \\ + 34 \\ \hline \end{array}$$
$$\begin{array}{r} 62 \\ + 18 \\ \hline \end{array}$$
$$\begin{array}{r} 78 \\ + 7 \\ \hline \end{array}$$
$$\begin{array}{r} 59 \\ + 24 \\ \hline \end{array}$$

3.
$$\begin{array}{r} 67 \\ + 18 \\ \hline \end{array}$$
$$\begin{array}{r} 56 \\ + 24 \\ \hline \end{array}$$
$$\begin{array}{r} 29 \\ + 58 \\ \hline \end{array}$$
$$\begin{array}{r} 45 \\ + 35 \\ \hline \end{array}$$

4.
$$\begin{array}{r} 76 \\ + 18 \\ \hline \end{array}$$
$$\begin{array}{r} 54 \\ + 27 \\ \hline \end{array}$$
$$\begin{array}{r} 43 \\ + 49 \\ \hline \end{array}$$
$$\begin{array}{r} 87 \\ + 8 \\ \hline \end{array}$$

Practice Adding Tens and Ones

Add the following equations.

Swordfish

1.
$$59 + 7$$ $$74 + 15$$ $$85 + 7$$ $$76 + 12$$

2.
$$70 + 19$$ $$66 + 23$$ $$48 + 23$$ $$27 + 8$$

3.
$$88 + 7$$ $$40 + 28$$ $$75 + 17$$ $$29 + 65$$

How many miles can these
animals swim in an hour?

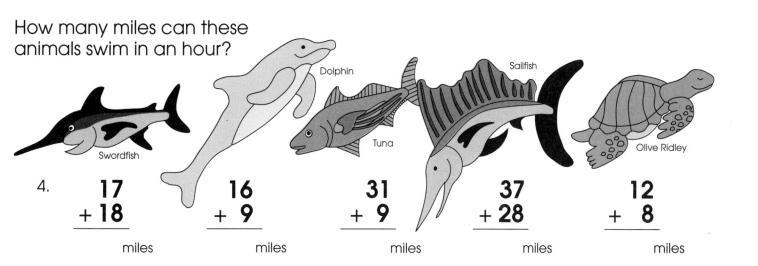

Dolphin   Sailfish

Swordfish   Tuna   Olive Ridley

4.
$$17 + 18$$ $$16 + 9$$ $$31 + 9$$ $$37 + 28$$ $$12 + 8$$

_____ miles   _____ miles   _____ miles   _____ miles   _____ miles

Subtracting Tens and Ones Using Renaming

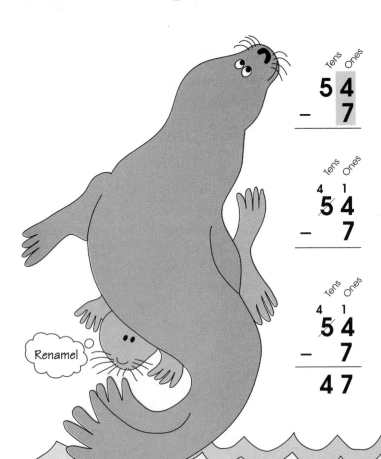

Rename!

	Tens	Ones
	5	4
−		7

1. Start with the ones.
   4 − 7 **cannot** be done!
   You must **rename**.

	Tens	Ones
	⁴5	¹4
−		7

2. Take one ten from the tens.
   10 + 4 = 14 in the ones.
   5 − 1 = 4 in the tens.

	Tens	Ones
	⁴5	¹4
−		7
	4	7

3. Now subtract.
   Ones first.   14 − 7 = 7
   Now the **tens**.   4 − 0 = 4

Now it's your turn to subtract.
Be sure to **rename**.

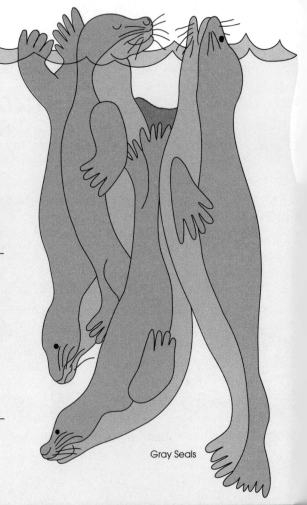

Gray Seals

	Tens	Ones			
1.	5	3	6	5	9	2
	−	6	− 8		− 4

1. 53 − 6   65 − 8   92 − 4

2. 44 − 8   78 − 9   21 − 5

Subtraction Using Renaming

Subtract to find the difference for each equation.
Be sure to **rename**.

1.
$$\begin{array}{r} 54 \\ -\ 7 \\ \hline \end{array}$$
$$\begin{array}{r} 67 \\ -\ 8 \\ \hline \end{array}$$
$$\begin{array}{r} 82 \\ -\ 5 \\ \hline \end{array}$$
$$\begin{array}{r} 40 \\ -\ 6 \\ \hline \end{array}$$

2.
$$\begin{array}{r} 22 \\ -\ 4 \\ \hline \end{array}$$
$$\begin{array}{r} 95 \\ -\ 7 \\ \hline \end{array}$$
$$\begin{array}{r} 73 \\ -\ 8 \\ \hline \end{array}$$
$$\begin{array}{r} 36 \\ -\ 7 \\ \hline \end{array}$$

3.
$$\begin{array}{r} 48 \\ -\ 29 \\ \hline \end{array}$$
$$\begin{array}{r} 50 \\ -\ 25 \\ \hline \end{array}$$
$$\begin{array}{r} 26 \\ -\ 17 \\ \hline \end{array}$$
My name is Fred!
$$\begin{array}{r} 34 \\ -\ 25 \\ \hline \end{array}$$

Who's larger?

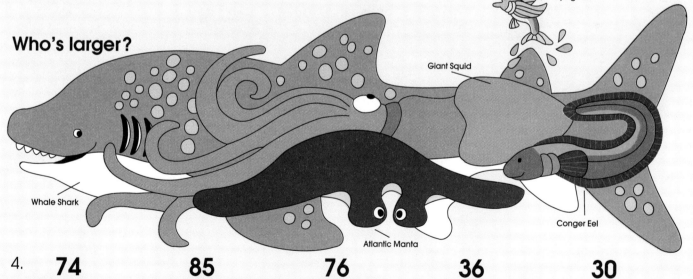

Flying Fish

Giant Squid

Whale Shark

Atlantic Manta

Conger Eel

4.
$$\begin{array}{r} 74 \\ -\ 19 \\ \hline \end{array}$$
feet
$$\begin{array}{r} 85 \\ -\ 38 \\ \hline \end{array}$$
feet
$$\begin{array}{r} 76 \\ -\ 58 \\ \hline \end{array}$$
feet
$$\begin{array}{r} 36 \\ -\ 27 \\ \hline \end{array}$$
feet
$$\begin{array}{r} 30 \\ -\ 29 \\ \hline \end{array}$$
foot

Whale Shark	Giant Squid	Atlantic Manta	Conger Eel	Flying Fish

Subtraction Practice

Write the **difference** to each subtraction equation.

1.
$$\begin{array}{r} 57 \\ -\ 9 \\ \hline \end{array}$$
$$\begin{array}{r} 24 \\ -10 \\ \hline \end{array}$$
$$\begin{array}{r} 36 \\ -17 \\ \hline \end{array}$$
$$\begin{array}{r} 82 \\ -66 \\ \hline \end{array}$$

2.
$$\begin{array}{r} 75 \\ -23 \\ \hline \end{array}$$
$$\begin{array}{r} 43 \\ -18 \\ \hline \end{array}$$
$$\begin{array}{r} 61 \\ -56 \\ \hline \end{array}$$
$$\begin{array}{r} 40 \\ -27 \\ \hline \end{array}$$

3.
$$\begin{array}{r} 94 \\ -58 \\ \hline \end{array}$$
$$\begin{array}{r} 38 \\ -\ 9 \\ \hline \end{array}$$
$$\begin{array}{r} 88 \\ -78 \\ \hline \end{array}$$
$$\begin{array}{r} 55 \\ -27 \\ \hline \end{array}$$

4.
$$\begin{array}{r} 18 \\ -\ 6 \\ \hline \end{array}$$
$$\begin{array}{r} 44 \\ -17 \\ \hline \end{array}$$
$$\begin{array}{r} 70 \\ -35 \\ \hline \end{array}$$
$$\begin{array}{r} 39 \\ -19 \\ \hline \end{array}$$

Sea Otter

Addition and Subtraction Practice

Find the **sum** or the **difference** for each equation. Be careful!

1.
$$45 + 35$$
$$89 - 62$$
$$36 - 18$$
$$72 + 18$$

2.
$$50 - 25$$
$$65 + 28$$
$$91 + 8$$
$$25 + 25$$

3.
$$32 + 48$$
$$49 + 37$$
$$74 - 28$$
$$19 - 17$$

4.
$$88 - 66$$
$$36 + 36$$
$$67 - 18$$
$$91 - 19$$

Adding Hundreds, Tens and Ones

1. Add the **ones first**.
2. Add the **tens second**.
3. Add the **hundreds last**.

1. Add the **ones**. **Regroup** to **tens**.
2. Add the **tens** plus the **new ten**.
3. Add the **hundreds**.

Hundreds Tens Ones

```
  5 3 4
+ 2 5 3
-------
  7 8 7
```

Hundreds Tens Ones

```
    1
  6 2 7
+ 1 5 5
-------
  7 8 2
```

Find the **sum** for each equation.

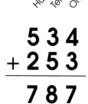

1.
```
  547
+ 345
-----
```
```
  136
+ 546
-----
```
```
  481
+ 209
-----
```

2.
```
  628
+ 167
-----
```
```
  287
+ 707
-----
```
```
  345
+ 248
-----
```

3.
```
  407
+ 486
-----
```
```
  524
+ 127
-----
```
```
  753
+ 118
-----
```

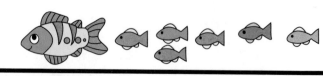

Adding Hundreds, Tens and Ones

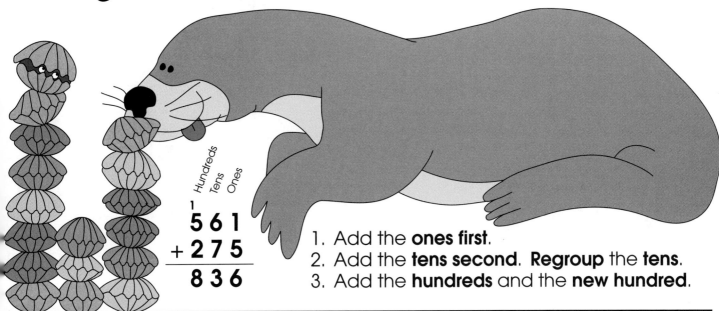

$$\begin{array}{r} \overset{1}{5}\ 6\ 1 \\ +\ 2\ 7\ 5 \\ \hline 8\ 3\ 6 \end{array}$$

Hundreds Tens Ones

1. Add the **ones first**.
2. Add the **tens second**. **Regroup** the **tens**.
3. Add the **hundreds** and the **new hundred**.

Find the **sum** for each equation.

1.
$$\begin{array}{r} 584 \\ +\ 372 \\ \hline \end{array}$$
$$\begin{array}{r} 240 \\ +\ 495 \\ \hline \end{array}$$
$$\begin{array}{r} 798 \\ +\ 114 \\ \hline \end{array}$$

2.
$$\begin{array}{r} 591 \\ +\ 147 \\ \hline \end{array}$$
$$\begin{array}{r} 278 \\ +\ 243 \\ \hline \end{array}$$
$$\begin{array}{r} 632 \\ +\ 287 \\ \hline \end{array}$$

3.
$$\begin{array}{r} 745 \\ +\ 187 \\ \hline \end{array}$$
$$\begin{array}{r} 188 \\ +\ 181 \\ \hline \end{array}$$
$$\begin{array}{r} 276 \\ +\ 575 \\ \hline \end{array}$$

Subtracting Hundreds, Tens and Ones

1. Subtract the ones.
You must **rename**!

```
      Hundreds
         Tens
            Ones
        6  1
     5  7̸  6
  -  2  2  8
  _____
     3  4  8
```

2. Subtract the **ones**.
3. Subtract the **tens**.
4. Subtract the **hundreds**.

Find the **difference** for each equation.

1.
$$574 - 458$$ $$356 - 149$$ $$825 - 207$$

2.
$$756 - 348$$ $$473 - 158$$ $$392 - 347$$

3.
$$864 - 508$$ $$615 - 208$$ $$973 - 755$$

Addition and Subtraction Practice

Find the **sum** or **difference** for each equation.

Sei Whale

1.
$$585 - 269$$
$$274 + 234$$
$$108 + 544$$

2.
$$922 - 108$$
$$184 + 507$$
$$355 - 118$$

3.
$$571 + 262$$
$$963 - 125$$
$$456 + 138$$

4.
$$222 - 115$$
$$753 + 156$$
$$151 - 138$$

Humpback Whale

Addition and Subtraction

Put an **X** on each incorrect answer.
Which seal has the most correct answers?

_____

$$\begin{array}{r} 64 \\ + 23 \\ \hline 97 \end{array} \qquad \begin{array}{r} 36 \\ + 27 \\ \hline 63 \end{array} \qquad \begin{array}{r} 387 \\ + 116 \\ \hline 493 \end{array}$$

$$\begin{array}{r} 84 \\ - 36 \\ \hline 98 \end{array} \qquad \begin{array}{r} 73 \\ - 27 \\ \hline 46 \end{array} \qquad \begin{array}{r} 460 \\ - 129 \\ \hline 342 \end{array}$$

$$\begin{array}{r} 39 \\ + 25 \\ \hline 64 \end{array} \qquad \begin{array}{r} 47 \\ + 35 \\ \hline 82 \end{array} \qquad \begin{array}{r} 392 \\ + 138 \\ \hline 530 \end{array}$$

$$\begin{array}{r} 79 \\ - 34 \\ \hline 35 \end{array} \qquad \begin{array}{r} 83 \\ - 36 \\ \hline 47 \end{array} \qquad \begin{array}{r} 467 \\ - 138 \\ \hline 329 \end{array}$$

$$\begin{array}{r} 39 \\ + 27 \\ \hline 66 \end{array} \qquad \begin{array}{r} 44 \\ + 38 \\ \hline 86 \end{array} \qquad \begin{array}{r} 384 \\ + 127 \\ \hline 511 \end{array}$$

$$\begin{array}{r} 88 \\ - 39 \\ \hline 49 \end{array} \qquad \begin{array}{r} 60 \\ - 27 \\ \hline 33 \end{array} \qquad \begin{array}{r} 452 \\ - 137 \\ \hline 325 \end{array}$$

Answer Key

Page 1
1. 5 + 3 = 8
2. 3 + 6 = 9
3. 4 + 4 = 8
4. 6 + 2 = 8
5. 4 + 5 = 9
6. 3 + 7 = 10
7. 7 + 2 = 9

Page 2
1. 6, 4, 10
2. 2, 12, 16
3. 8, 14, 18
4. 12, 6, 2
5. 4, 8, 14

Page 3
1. 9, 3, 7
2. 13, 5, 17
3. 15, 7, 13
4. 17, 9, 5
5. 3, 13, 17

Page 4
1. 6, 7, 10
2. 11, 14, 15
3. 8, 9, 16
4. 17, 5, 12
5. 13, 18, 15

Page 5

10	11	12
5 + 5	5 + 6	6 + 6
4 + 6	8 + 3	
	4 + 7	

13	14	15
6 + 7	8 + 6	9 + 6
4 + 9	9 + 5	7 + 8
10 + 3	7 + 7	10 + 5
	4 + 10	

Page 6
1. 11, 11, 14, 14
2. 11, 11, 17, 17
3. 13, 13, 13, 13
4. 10, 10, 12, 12
5. 13, 13, 15, 15
6. 12, 12, 11, 11
7. 16, 16, 9, 9

Page 7
Starfish
Clockwise from arrow
10, 13, 11, 15, 14

Snail
Down from arrow
13, 12, 11, 14

Turtle
Clockwise from arrow
13, 10, 16, 12, 15, 14

Jellyfish
Left to Right from arrow
13, 15, 16, 17

Page 8
1. 15, 16, 17, 15
2. 17, 14, 11, 18
3. 11, 15, 15, 17

Page 9
1. 11 - 5 = 6
2. 10 - 7 = 3
3. 15 - 8 = 7
4. 12 - 6 = 6
5. 12 - 5 = 7
6. 10 - 6 = 4
7. 11 - 8 = 3

Page 10

13	14
4 + 9 = 13	8 + 6 = 14
9 + 4 = 13	6 + 8 = 14
13 - 4 = 9	14 - 8 = 6
13 - 9 = 4	14 - 6 = 8

15	16	17
8 + 7 = 15	9 + 7 = 16	8 + 9 = 17
7 + 8 = 15	7 + 9 = 16	9 + 8 = 17
15 - 8 = 7	16 - 9 = 7	17 - 8 = 9
15 - 7 = 8	16 - 7 = 9	17 - 9 = 8

Page 11
1. 7, 9, 6, 7, 9
2. 5, 8, 5, 8, 7
3. 6, 7, 8, 5, 7

Page 12
1. 12, 8, 7
2. 8, 13, 8
3. 9, 15, 9
4. 15, 13, 12, 4, 9
5. 8, 6, 12, 8, 8

Page 13
1. 10, 8, 8, 6, 6
2. 9, 7, 7, 7, 11
3. 5, 8, 10
4. 3, 6, 9

Page 14
1. 10, 11, 17
2. 4, 9, 7
3. 7, 9, 10
4. 5, 6, 6

	Subtract 5	Add 6	Subtract 7	Add 8
	5	14	7	14
	8	11	8	16
	6	15	4	19
	9	13	2	17

Answer Key

Page 15
1. 67, 99, 55
2. 79, 28, 89
3. 79, 97, 86
4. 98, 109, 69

Page 16
G86, C96, T78, W94
A95, J97, R99, G64
U81, E59, H66, L68
W77, L25, E70, B49
BLUE WHALE

Page 17
1. 55, 42, 62
2. 73, 21, 92
3. 25, 23, 63
4. 36, 42, 52

Page 18
1. 32, 84, 43
2. 37, 31, 21
3. 23, 31, 22
4. 33, 72, 7
5. 19, 42, 85

Page 19
1. 63, 33, 92
2. 32, 52, 44
3. 62, 56, 70

Page 20
1. 62, 31, 40, 81
2. 82, 80, 85, 83
3. 85, 80, 87, 80
4. 94, 81, 92, 95

Page 21
1. 66, 89, 92, 88
2. 89, 89, 71, 35
3. 95, 68, 92, 94
4. 35, 25, 40, 65, 20

Page 22
1. 47, 57, 88
2. 36, 69, 16

Page 23
1. 47, 59, 77, 34
2. 18, 88, 65, 29
3. 19, 25, 9, 9
4. 55, 47, 18, 9, 1

Page 24
1. 48, 14, 19, 16
2. 52, 25, 5, 13
3. 36, 29, 10, 28
4. 12, 27, 35, 20

Page 25
1. 80, 27, 18, 90
2. 25, 93, 99, 50
3. 80, 86, 46, 2
4. 22, 72, 49, 72

Page 26
1. 892, 682, 690
2. 795, 994, 593
3. 893, 651, 871

Page 27
1. 956, 735, 912
2. 738, 521, 919
3. 932, 369, 851

Page 28
1. 116, 207, 618
2. 408, 315, 45
3. 356, 407, 218

Page 29
1. 316, 508, 652
2. 814, 691, 237
3. 833, 838, 594
4. 107, 909, 13

Page 30
1. 97 (87), 63, 493(503), 98 (48),
   46, 342 (331)
2. 64, 82, 530, 35 (45), 47, 329
3. 66, 86 (82), 511, 49, 33, 325 (315)
SEAL 2

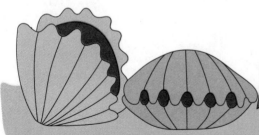
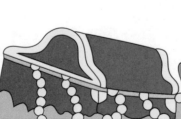
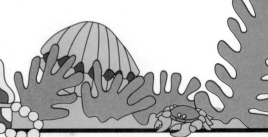